IRRITATING THE SILVER LINING

Published by New Generation Publishing in 2022

All poems and photographs copyright © Dave Kurley 2022

First Edition

The author asserts the moral right under the Copyright, Designs and Patents Act 1988 to be identified as the author of this work.

All Rights reserved. No part of this publication may be reproduced, stored in a retrieval system or transmitted, in any form or by any means without the prior consent of the author, nor be otherwise circulated in any form of binding or cover other than that which it is published and without a similar condition being imposed on the subsequent purchaser.

Paperback: 978-1-80369-427-6
Ebook: 978-1-80369-428-3

www.newgeneration-publishing.com

New Generation Publishing

Irritating the Silver Lining

Poems and Photographs

Dave Kurley

What they're saying about @kurleybobspoetrycorner

(Reviews of Dave Kurley's poetry pages on Facebook and Instagram)

...you see the extraordinary in the ordinary and put the ordinary into the otherworldly Gryphaea Arcuata

To read Dave's poetry is to purchase a ticket to the cinema of his mind. And it's in IMAX. Brad Dunn

A poem a day to challenge your thinking, to make you smile, to make you wonder and might even make you cry
Sharon Ellis

Poetry you can touch with your fingers, smell with your nose and hear in your ears, each verse, a new journey of words, to walk alongside.
Flo Jo Flanders

Wise and witty, full of memories, and meanderings, clever quips and cunning clips, thoughtful and thorough, sad and sorrowful, funny and fabulous...in fact everything you need to read...in a poem a day!
Katie Greathead

Poetry for those who think they don't like poetry
Jayne Kerr

I've always enjoyed the unusual use of words. The way they make you think, the way they make you smile or laugh out loud. The way they make you cry. The way they scare you or the way they wrap around you. You are the best wordsmith xxx
Pat Kurley

Dave is one of the nicest blokes I've ever had the pleasure to meet. I'd read anything he'd write but I'm glad it's poetry and not erotic fan-fiction
Ashley Linegar

Imaginative, funny, frightening and evocative!
Rosemary Morton

I like the ritual of it, seeing something, from you, every day. And sharing the pleasure, with you, of using the words to make pictures and stories.
Scarlett Shimwell

Unpretentious poetry for ordinary people - Who knew I'd know a poet?!?
Kathryn Wilkinson

Poetry you won't want to put down
Phoenix Wright

Take a trip around the mind of the indomitable wordsmith who goes by the name of Dave Kurley to enjoy his perfectly perfect poetry!
Shirley Young

Contents

Preface	ix
Foreword	xi
Morning	1
I Told You There Was a Wolf	2
Disturbed	4
The Difficult Patient, part one	5
Abundance	6
Brothers Corvo	8
Poets' Estate	9
The Difficult Patient, part two	10
Missing the Moment	11
All the Swearwords	12
Hot Monster	13
The Difficult Patient, part three	14
Irritating the Silver Lining	15
Post-Industrial	16
Idling	17
The Difficult Patient, part four	18
Impressions of a Video Seen on The Guardian Website, July 2021	19
The Height of Summer	20
Withering-by-the-Sea	21
The Difficult Patient, part five	22
Impressions of the Pedrógão Grande Fire, June 2017	23
Deconstruction	24
St. Simeon's Acolytes	25
The Difficult Patient, part six	26
The Inconstancy of Memory	27

Buying Time	28
Stubborn Dusk	29
The Difficult Patient, part seven	30
Big Orange Quiet Sky	31
It's Not Like Withering-by-the-Sea	32
Silent Reflection	33
The Difficult Patient, Sidebar: About Desmond	34
Dark Presses Down	36
Unfamiliar	37
Appointment With Fear	38
The Difficult Patient, part eight	40
Vixen, Captured	41
Summat in Miss Dale's Classroom	42
Burnt-Out Life	46
The Difficult Patient, part nine	47
Dizzy Heights	48
inbetween	49
Moita Negra Midwinter Night	50
The Difficult Patient, part ten	51
Shot	52
The Optimist	53
A Gentle Legacy	54
The Difficult Patient, part eleven	55
She Flies Alone	56
Still There	57
Quinta da Silva	58
The Difficult Patient, Season Finale	62
The Party's Over	64
What Do We Leave Behind?	65
I've Been Out	66
Without Words	67
Acknowledgements	68

Preface

This is what happened.

After years of talking about moving to a different country (for the adventure, for something to do, for something), in 2016, Alison and I finally took the plunge and relocated to the slowly beating heart of central Portugal...

...and for a couple of years, we ran a glamping site here, but an uninvited hurricane had a wild party in the valley one October weekend and ruined it for everybody.

So that didn't work out, but we stayed in Portugal, because by this time, our hearts were here, and we filled our days teaching conversational English online to people all over the world, and exploring our adopted home...

...and we were thinking about maybe spending some time touring further afield, round Europe maybe, or even other continents, when an uninvited pandemic had a wild party everywhere for a couple of years and really ruined it for everybody.

Now, back in the day, I did a bit of writing (lyrics for the band I sang with, scripts for stand-up comedy, a couple of plays, an unpublished novel), and I still wrote the odd (very odd) haiku. And thanks to Kate Hull Rodgers and her online writing workshop, I found my muse in the middle of a pandemic...

...and since New Year's Day 2021, I've been writing a poem every day and posting them on Instagram and Facebook (@kurleybobspoetrycorner), using my own photos, sometimes as inspiration, sometimes as illustration...

...and a selection of them is what you're holding in your hand.

In here, there's stuff about memory, nature, observations about my old home town of Sheffield and the contrast between suburban existence back there and the bucolic life we lead now in central Portugal. And holding it all unsteadily together is the strange tale of The Difficult Patient...

...and there are links between the various pieces that I'm sure you'll be able to fathom. If you can't (or indeed, can't be bothered), it doesn't matter. It's not an exam.

Are you ready? Yes? Excellent. Let's get started.

Dave Kurley
Moita Negra, Portugal
May 2022

Foreword

I first met Dave a dozen years ago. My husband, Bill, announced that we were having a couple of friends visit. Dave and his lovely wife, Ali. Who are they? I queried. I was assured that they were old friends. I thought to myself that Bill and I had been married a dozen years and I had never heard of Dave or Ali. They came to visit, we went to the pub for lunch. And laugh, I could have cried we laughed so much and so hard. Dave and Ali instantly became old friends to me even though I had only known them an hour.

The next time I met Dave was a few years later. He and his band came to play at a charity event that Bill was organising. I looked forward to seeing him. He and his band seemed a jovial lot. But I truly knew they were my kind of people when they found some make up and for a lark they painted their faces to look like Kiss. I danced the night away to Dave's fabulous singing and the band's raucous tunes.

Roll forward to the beginning of the pandemic. I, like so much of the world, was in a state of panic. But then Bill came up with the idea that I could present some classes online. I duly set up an online writing workshop. I called it "Don't get it Right, Get it Written" in the hope that I would attract some non-writers that I could teach. Imagine my surprise and my delight when at the first class Dave Kurley tuned in.

Over the next few weeks Dave proved to be an avid writer and each week he became more adventurous. About the same time I began to see Dave's wonderful undertaking called Kurleybob's Poetry Corner on social media. It began with Dave reading poems to celebrate birthdays but it quickly turned into a marvellous offering each day.

New Years of 2021 came. In class I asked the writers if they had any resolutions. Imagine my delight when Dave announced he would write a poem a day for a year. Good luck with that one!

I was extremely impressed when, there on Facebook, every day, was the result of Dave's hard work. Not only a poem, but a photograph. This was marvellous stuff. The year of 2021 has passed, but Dave has not stopped writing. Every day, a new poem.

It didn't take long for Dave to realise that these poems belonged in a book. And that, of course, is what you hold in your hands. What started as a challenge has become a brilliant endeavour.

I 'see' Dave once a week for our writing workshop and every week he has seven poems under his belt. I admire his dedication and his tenacity. Not to mention how much I admire his poetry.

Enjoy the book, a new poet has been born. He is prolific and talented. Long may he produce.

Kate Hull Rodgers

Author and International Speaker

For the CFO

...and for MIllhouse

Morning

The dawn chorus is between verses
Beaks agape, bubblegum tongues balled
The trains are between stations
Silent and unlit in the sidings
Tides are poised above shores
Waves curl, do not crash
The earth is between breaths
Wait for it

In the thick of thin white light
Silvery layers of stillness
A heart between beats
Anticipates the arrival

Of morning

I Told You There Was a Wolf

I told you there was a wolf
I told you all
And you wanted proof
You wanted to see the spoor
'Show us the carcasses', you said.
'Give us pictures from the cameras that never lie.'
But the wolf was clever
It cleaned up after itself
Created false trails
It was forensically careful.
But I knew it was there,
Waiting
Biding its time.
I told Grandma there was a wolf
She didn't believe at first
But I was persistent,
Supplied argument and counterargument:
I won her round.
And she had sympathetic friends at the home
And then -
And then, one late, silverlit night in her room
The wolf came in and ate her
Took her voice
Convinced her friends it didn't exist
And ate them
One by one
And the carers, too
Until the home was empty
Except for the wolf
Grinning from the high windows
And nobody visited the home anymore
So the wolf went to the woods
I went to the Town Hall
Told the Mayor
Told him about the wolf
And what became of my Grandma
And her friends
And the carers

And now -
And now the wolf was in the woods
Waiting
Biding its time
And the Mayor said:
'What do you want me to do?
Put guards round the woods?
People picnic in the woods.
People buy food from the grocers
To picnic in those woods.
If the people can't picnic in our woods
They'll picnic elsewhere
And what will happen to the town
With no picnic money?
What do you want me to do?
Put guards round the woods?'
'Yes!' I said. 'Put guards round the woods.
Fence the woods off
A no-go area.
Starve the wolf.'
But the Mayor wouldn't do those things
And the people picnicked in the woods
And the wolf picnicked on the people
One by one
Even the Mayor
And his wife
And their kids
(They were there for the publicity shots)
The wolf ate them all
One by one
Ate them
Every one
All gone
Just me now
I daren't go out
The wolf waits.

                                                  I told you there was a wolf
                                                        I told you all.

Disturbed

It's bad enough that they kept me awake
All last night with their carousing
He thought as he glared at his muesli
Sadly soggy with semi-skimmed,
Sorrowfully sweetened with stevia, not sugar

Bad enough I could hear every word
Of their too-loud, top volume conversation
Continuing through the early hours with their laughter:
Now I have to suffer the re-runs,
The self-congratulatory nostalgia
For last night's frolics and debauchery. Good grief!
They stole in next door noisily late and thieved
A full five hours' sleep from me
And now, unknowing, unapologetic
They sit next to me with their terrible good moods
Unhungover, unaware of the damage,
Their decimation of my day -

And this muesli is like the sweepings
From the bottom of a budgie's birdcage
I am not having a good morning
Don't you dare 'good morning' me.

The Difficult Patient, part one

This is how it happened:
She saw the job in her local paper
Fresh out of nursing college
And looking for work
Long before her hair became flecked with grey

And when the interviewer said:
'He's quite the difficult customer, is Mr Draper
Many nurses have come and gone in the past
What makes you different?
What makes you think you'll last?'
'Simple,' she answered. 'I never give up.
I never give in. Just ask me mother.
If Mr Draper's the immovable object
I'm the unstoppable force
And I'll move him, one way or another.'

She wasn't the first nurse
To marry her patient
And she probably wouldn't be the last
She had looked after him for
God knows how long
And even after all this time
His fingernail grip on life
Was still surprisingly strong.

Abundance

There is abundance in the bright air
Intoxicated borboletas
Stagger, wobble and flutter
Through the blue
From bud to blossom to bloom
Uncurling an unfeasible tongue
Desperately questing, prodding,
dipping, diving
One last slurp of sweetness
One for the shining road.

Homebuilding hoopoes hunting down hair,
Haphazard wainscoting for cracks in cliffs
To house their noxious, noisome chicks
Grasping grapnel beaks agape for arachnids
Happy, safe and secure in their own muck.
The solemn nonsense of their mother's call
Is echoed by her permanent punk surprise.

There is abundance in the forest morning.
Hordes of orchids:
Early purple, naked man, three toothed,
Serried ranks of Kerry lilies,
Flotillas of Scilla monophyllus,
German chamomile and crocus-leaved romulea.
Some names, exotic or everyday,
Words outside experience
Were uncovered here, my sylvan education
Mere footsteps from the middle of nowhere.

The forest doesn't recognise or intuit
This complicated taxonomy,
This human need for naming,
Just gets on with the job of
Encouraging, coaching
Abundance.

Abundance

There is abundance in my hometown too
But it is not always obvious
Dusky russet foxes lope down backstreets
Scenting the food bins behind trendy-ish restaurants
Effecting an almost mindful, dog-like posture
Before leaping in headlong
And munching on some foetid, thrownaway tidbits

How different
Are the defiant sparrowhawks
Butchering topheavy woodpigeons
Slack and unfeathered
In neat and oppressively hedged back gardens
While fat rats scavenge sunflower seeds
Burgled from the aluminium-perched feeders
(Where woodpigeons once gorged)
By dedicatedly opportunistic squirrels.

The forest busts out unexpectedly
The stark determination of buddleia,
Seeking bare sustenance between the bricks
Of timeworn workshop outbuildings
Pinky-purple panicles triumphantly beckon butterflies
To drink deep, flashes of brightness in the post-industrial wastes
Yes, there is abundance
But it is easily missed.

Brothers Corvo

Glossy gleaming Brothers Corvo
Wherever there's one, the other one goes
Shadowing, twinning Brothers Crow

Soaring screaming Brothers Corvo
To the tipmost tallest treetops they float
Lustrous, nightwinged Brothers Crow

Bright-eyed beaming Brothers Corvo
Foraging for wriggly or rancid chow
Peckish, ravenous Brothers Crow

Black Lane ends
Between Wordsworth
And Tennyson
Between Shelley and Kipling.
Yours are By-ways.
Now that side of the road is cleared
And former backworks erased
And further up the road, where once a pub stood, but is not now
Still there.
You probably don't remember that.
There are whispered memories
Where former pubs offer
In another borough
Were Shakespeare
Had Osgerby Meeting-boards
First colonised
Then demolished
Now erased.
Over the crest of Adlington (also not a poet)
Lies Southey Green – now Southey, he was a poet.
Wrote Inchcape Rock, amongst others, but
He was not from Sheffield.

On Southey Green Road once was a pub
Drawing in a mist
A Top Rib-house
The Mooney shop break there
Where in the sky
Are your branches full of
The flourished bouquet
Over what was to be car park
Standing as a suitcase
So we could look out for the cops.
Now as a car lot,
Social history buried beneath
Like Richard the Third in Leicester.
Not far from here is my house
On another road that is not named after a poet.
They call it the Poets' Estate,
Even though
Not all the avenues, closes, roads and crescents
Are named after poets.

For Chris

The Difficult Patient, part two

It was true, what the interviewer had said
They'd all thrown the soiled towel in
Every one of them, sooner or later
And with good reason
Mr Draper wasn't exactly adorable
He had all the warmth of an abandoned abattoir
His demeanour, in general, was deplorable
As charming as a decomposing badger

But she won him over
The awful things he'd said to her predecessors
The screaming monologues of hoarse invective
The uneaten meals hurled against the walls
The sodden bedsheets and the hideous messes
He left in the commode
Were all taken in her smiling stride

No matter how hard he tried to unhinge her
It would be: 'Oh Mr Draper! Such a tart tongue you have!'
Or 'Did you not like the curry? Was it the ginger?'
Or 'Oh dear - did you sleep in this? Poor Mr Draper!'

All the tools he had at his disposal
Ground the others down to dust
But they only served to polish her, make her shine
And there was no way she was going to give up.

And one morning, peering lizardly over his paper
He asked her: 'Have you ever bet on the horses?'
She smiled. 'Me mother was keen on the gee-gees -
She took me to several of the county's courses.
So, do you fancy a flutter, Mr Draper?'

Missing the Moment

Sometimes
We are so intent on
Capturing the moment that
We miss it and
Have instead to
Rely upon the
Faulty recollection of beauty in
Our own imperfect memories

All the Swearwords

I was probably five years old
When Mark Adams taught me all the swearwords
All of them
Every one.
He was sure of this, because his older brothers
Told him so.
The pair of us sat, curled kids in concrete pipes
Cemented into one corner of the beige concrete playground
Under a huge bruise of a thunderstormy sky
With Mark reciting all the swearwords to me
One by one
And as he solemnly announced each swearword
I repeated them, with equal solemnity.
What we did that afternoon playtime was arcane,
Esoteric, staggeringly important
There was a dark, magical intensity
To all of these taboo expressions
They were little hymns to the God of cursewords
And as the storm hit
We ran hell for leather
Round the playground, screaming
A litany of obscenity as lightning
Backlit the looming silhouette of the school building
And cold rain extinguished the burning profanity
Of the terrible, exciting words I had learned
It was a profound epiphany of rudeness
And I sometimes wonder
What were those words?
Fifty-odd years on, I couldn't tell you
But I remember learning each one.

Hot Monster

And the earth shudders and spews
An arc of glowing, burning death
The pressure increases like a blister
Like a thumb over a hose
And hissing up and round and down
A deadly pyrogenic Catherine Wheel
Molten Day-Glo pink and peach
Splattering and spattering, belching and bubbling
Sizzling and spitting through the beach to the terrified sea

This island should not behave like this
It should be neat rows of idyllic sunbrellas
Ordered plantations bursting full of
Fat little bananas
Second homes with high-ceilinged bedrooms
And beautiful vistas of the valley
And the vast ocean beyond

But no

The earth groans, shifts, and vomits
A thick stream of incandescent stuff
Chucks out three storey rocks like they're polystyrene
And under and over and round it all
The steady, relentless jet scream of eruption
The roar of the hot monster beneath.

The Difficult Patient, part three

Now Mr Draper had been, for many years
The talk of the local bookies
His skill at picking the wrong horse was legendary
So much so, they were known as 'Draper's donkeys'

But his nurse changed all that
She had a knack for the nags
And slowly but surely
Luck's tide turned for Mr Draper
And his penny wagers turned into pound after pound
And at her urging, his betting habits became more complex
Accumulators, Yankees and even Goliaths
And never lost, leaving the bookmakers perplexed

So Mr Draper went
From an item, a morsel of idle gossip
To the scourge of the turf accountant

Nobody knew that behind the scenes
His nurse was his lucky charm
Who not only kept him clean
Made sure he popped his pills in a timely manner
Brought him breakfast, lunch and dinner
But also scanned the racing pages for him
And made selections - every one a winner!

And even though he was far older
He felt a twitch in his wrinkled heart
Was it love? Was it avarice?
Difficult to tell
But one morning he awoke
With a single thought on his mind
To change her status
From full-time nurse
To Draper, Mrs.

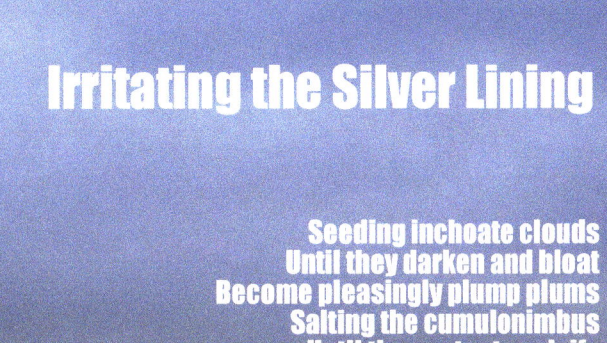

Irritating the Silver Lining

Seeding inchoate clouds
Until they darken and bloat
Become pleasingly plump plums
Salting the cumulonimbus
Until the contents calcify
And can no longer remain aloft
Irritating the silver lining
Until the sky weeps mother's pearls

Perfectly perfect, unblemished spheres
Precious hail for eager, grasping fingers
To pluck for punnets
From shattered windshields
Concave bonnets
And flayed allotments
After the beautiful glistening downpour.

Post-Industrial

These streets once echoed
With hobnail on cobble
And the clang of metal on metal
Now, a shortcut through decay
To a glittering palace of shopping.

Window with a patch on one eye
To help it grow, help it catch up
With its
Better-developed sibling

A sagging, fantailed blind
On the other
As if the shop has had a stroke
But still struggles into work
Because it has to
To survive.

Idling

The world runs slowly, out of gear
It is idling

No gondolas split the startling clarity of Venetian canals

The world sits in a Zoom room
With colour co-ordinated books
Stacked neatly behind
An affront to book readers everywhere
We tell the world
You're muted
We can't hear you
And your wi-fi signal is weak
Caught in an unflattering freeze
The world's image is
Idling

Sika deer stagger through a night club car park in the centre of Shanghai

The world stands
Masked, at a respectable distance
With clean hands
Outside a McDonalds
With its friends
Idling

Badgers amble, ticketless, across Sheffield station concourse

We ask our friends, colleagues, family
For news
There is no news
The world lolls in a hammock between two stocky pines
In the piercing, silent sun
Idling

River dolphins prod curious noses
Through the cold surface of the Yangtze

The world nearly stands still
Disengaged from its load
Idling

The Difficult Patient, part four

Hold on
Time out
This is all happening so fast
If caring for Mr Draper was her first job
And she was grey before they were wed
What happened in between times?
By the time they were due to be married
Surely he'd be long dead?

Good questions
But bear in mind
What you've seen so far
Has been a montage
Snapshots of memories
Vignettes and excerpts
Sketches and skits
Rather than the full picture
You wouldn't want to see the whole thing
Unexpurgated
Oh no

Suffice to say
Mr Draper was quite disturbingly old
And like the last guest at a party
Simply refused to leave
It's the main thing they had in common
Neither of them would ever give up

And just as an addendum
A tardy but welcome introduction
To a tenacious woman with a singular talent
Say hi to Imogen Smart
...soon to be Draper.

Impressions of a video seen on the Guardian website, July 2021

A stranded stranger with a cellphone testament
A 21st century memento malum

A river unknown
Pregnant with precipitous precipitation
Its waters break roughly, relentlessly
With a muscular gush
Through an unnamed German town

Overwhelmed by the sudden spate
Roads end without warning
Become weirs and waterfalls
Into unforeseen sinkholes
That appear, abrupt
With the dark magics
Of physics and geology
Or maybe long-disused mineworks - who knows?

The water, rushing, relentless
Bullying and grabbing and dragging and pushing
Sucking down and crushing
The civilised, ordered lives
Of friends neighbours and enemies alike
Into swirling, whirlpooling anarchy,
Unmaking solid, dependable homes
Unburdening the now filthy floors
Of furniture and and long-loved heirlooms
Unfixing the memories of whole families
The unbuilding of Heimat.

Swallowed by the dank, dirty deluge
The unstoppable torrent
And as entire streets collapse into chaos
A last wave
Goodbye.

The Height of Summer

Even at the height of summer
When the sun is brighter than the future
When the breeze up the valley
Is a warm and loving caress
You still miss them

Even with a full belly and half-lidded eyes
And a buzz from your favourite booze
And the loose handholding
As you lie together on the cool covers
Not awake, not asleep
You still miss them

The pull and sting of the unhealing scab that clings
Stubborn, to your resisting skin
The pull, the sting of separation never lessens
Is always there

Withering-by-the-Sea

The moon lurched up, late and louring
After another long, dull day
In Withering-by-the Sea
Where the sun only shines for a dare
Where the tide went out
Like a twenty watt bulb
Went out in lurid shame like a bad fashion choice
Like a cheap seaside entertainer
In a Donny Osmond hat
Swimming against the current
Off the coast of Withering-by-the Sea
Like a desperate corkscrew in search
Of a bottle of cheap Spanish red
Where the shells sit on the ungolden sands,
Unexploded
Get away from Withering-by-the Sea
Where a day trip is a bad trip
A holiday you'll always regret
You'll never forget it - for all the wrong reasons
Just get on the bus and for God's sake
Don't look back
Remember:
What happens in Withering
Will stay with you
For the rest of your miserable
And short life

The Difficult Patient, part five

How did Imogen know?
How did she pick the winners?
Was it an unforeseen result of her mum
Misspending her daughter's childhood
Gambling it away at all the county's courses:
At Beverley, Catterick, Doncaster,
Pontefract and Redcar,
Ripon, Thirsk and York?
Maybe it was
But this is not that story

How did Imogen do it?
How did she read the runners and riders
And instantly intuit all the places?
Was it a supernatural knack?
Was it clairvoyance
Or a precognitive flash?
Maybe at night she was visited
By a vision of her dear departed mother's ghost
Whispering the names of the firsts past the post
Perhaps
...but maybe she just knew.

Whatever the method
Whatever the origin
Imogen and Mr Draper
Were coining it in
Hand over reptilian fist
And all the bookies in town
Were physically sick from paying out
What scam was Draper pulling?
Was it something they'd missed?
They called a meet
In their favourite watering hole
The Hobby Horse and Green Man
To formulate a battle plan.

Impressions of the Pedrógão Grande Fire, June 2017

We are driving on hell's highway
To find friends and bring them back to somewhere safe
With charred and blackened pines
And smouldering eucalyptus embers
On either side.
Air heavy and blue-grey
With the bad memory of smoke
A slow dreadful journey through dark, billowing skies.

Pyrocumulonimbus
A fire-fuelled, fire breathing thunderstorm
Feeding on the flames
Randomly striking and spreading further flash fires
Thousands of acres burnt to the scrub
Four sleepless, unblinking days
Weeping through the smoke
Of infernal, blazing horror
Animals, wild and domestic
White-eyed, panicked, fleeing without direction
Families, villages, displaced, destroyed, devastated
The solitary comfort of the wilderness
Is lost beyond finding

Flames spring up where least expected
By roadside cafes hastily opened
To quench the thirsts of stranded motorists
We see burnt-out cars and skeletal vans
On grim pick-ups
And later we hear of the many dead
So many dead
On the terrible turn-off from hell's highway
Where on either side the forests are fuel
Where everything and everyone is fuel
Given enough heat.

Deconstruction

Lost in the moment
In his own little bubble
Between the ruin of a defunct edifice
And the genesis, the generation of rubble

Intent, unflinching
Reducing rusted rebar
With his hoarse roaring silver white flame
Shiva in a hard hat, creator, destroyer

St. Simeon's Acolytes

A flock of feathered ascetics
Aware and unaware, thoughts elsewhere
Stylites isolated on pillar and post
Meditating, contemplating fasting from fish
And the fleeting ecstasy
Of falling from some lofty perch
Then suddenly remembering
Wings

The Difficult Patient, part six

The Hobby Horse and Green Man
Was a nightmare 1960s Brutalist estate pub
With a concrete ski-slope roof
In the car park, 10-year-olds with muscles
Would threaten to beat you up
The shutters were always dragged down
Bomb-proof
Refusing to look out at the
Forgotten, misbegotten, rotten
Scrag end of town

The front door was never propped open
Not even in summer
The landlord reckoned it'd let all the muck in
And although he'd said things that were dumber
In a way, he wasn't that far from the truth

It was the perfect meeting place for the scheming bookies
Being the last place on earth anyone
Would ever feel lucky

They marched in, mob-handed, clad in balaclavas
Not through any pretence to menace
It was genuinely bitter outside and in
The landlord's hand was under the bar
On the 'porcelain persuader'
A spare beer pump handle ready for violence
But he stood down when they ordered ten pints of cider
And sat down in the snug
Plotting Draper's demise.

The Inconstancy of Memory

I don't remember where I was when Elvis died
I've been told that, at the age of fifteen
One day in August, 1977
I ran into my aunty's kitchen to tell her.
I do not remember this.
Later I remember seeing some skins in town
Taking the piss out of some Teddy Boys
In the Hole in the Road
Singing 'Elvis is dead! Elvis is dead!'

I remember where I was when Margaret Thatcher resigned
In a nondescript sales office in North Hendon
One day in November, 1990
I've been told that my mate Mick
Renamed one of the beers in his pub 'Iron Maiden'
Or something like that
I do not remember this.
There was much rejoicing
But my girlfriend at the time
Was less jubilant, warning that
This meant the Tories would get in again
And she was right.
We married a couple of years later.
I remember that.

When I was a kid
No more than seven or eight
I had quite a serious car accident
One day in April or May, 1970
I did the thing that all the adverts,
All the road safety lectures warn you about:
I walked out from behind an ice cream van
Without looking
Right into the path of a lumbering Ford Zephyr
I do not remember this
Everything about that day
I have been told by my mother
And my aunty
I don't actually remember anything about it

What I do remember
Is waking up in an uncomfortable, flat bed
Under a sizzling orange light
Feeling sick and dizzy
And staggering on cold feet
Out of my greenwalled, half-windowed room
Into a dark shiny floored corridor
Where a woman I didn't know
In a uniform like my mom's
Led me back into my room and into my bed.
She had warm hands
I remember that.

Buying Time

A golden shimmer illuminates the doorframe
Picks out the bare bones of the building
Dusts the floorboards of the balcony with precious metal luminance
Music pulses in a bloodbeat, pounding a bared chest
Showing out with easy love and sensual pride
Beating, beating
So chill, so warm, so sit down...
They smile, and we blink back, uncomprehending and then
Here we sit, with drinks of frozen sunshine
Buying time to save for later.

Stubborn Dusk

Stubborn, the light won't
Acknowledge the sun's retreat
Plays with the contrast
Adds silver to reflection
Silhouettes the horizon

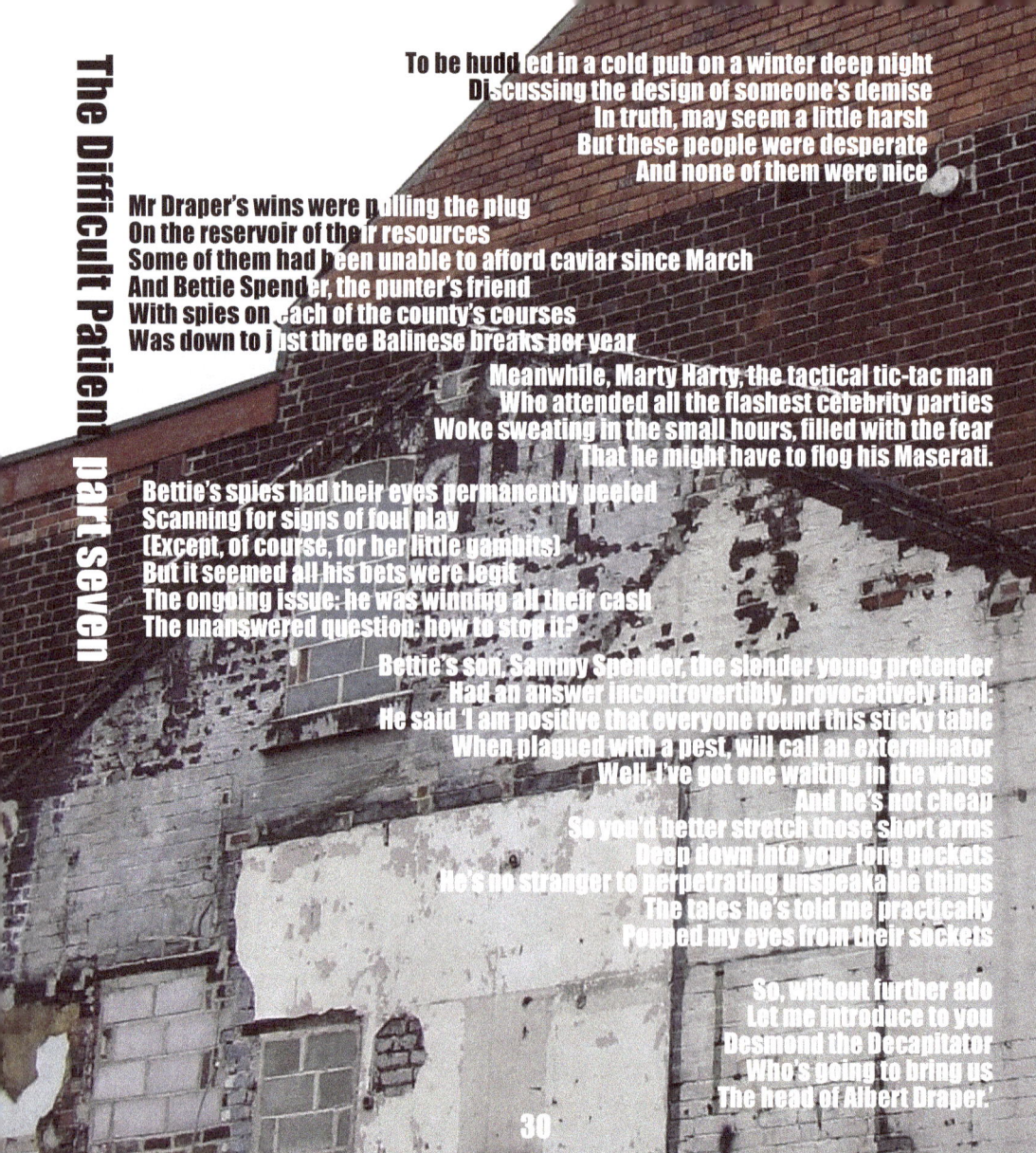

The Difficult Patient, part seven

                    To be huddled in a cold pub on a winter deep night
                      Discussing the design of someone's demise
                            In truth, may seem a little harsh
                        But these people were desperate
                          And none of them were nice

Mr Draper's wins were pulling the plug
On the reservoir of their resources
Some of them had been unable to afford caviar since March
And Bettie Spender, the punter's friend
With spies on each of the county's courses
Was down to just three Balinese breaks per year

                Meanwhile, Marty Harty, the tactical tic-tac man
                  Who attended all the flashest celebrity parties
                Woke sweating in the small hours, filled with the fear
                    That he might have to flog his Maserati.

Bettie's spies had their eyes permanently peeled
Scanning for signs of foul play
(Except, of course, for her little gambits)
But it seemed all his bets were legit
The ongoing issue: he was winning all their cash
The unanswered question: how to stop it?

              Bettie's son, Sammy Spender, the slender young pretender
              Had an answer incontrovertibly, provocatively final:
              He said 'I am positive that everyone round this sticky table
              When plagued with a pest, will call an exterminator
                Well, I've got one waiting in the wings
                        And he's not cheap
                So you'd better stretch those short arms
                  Deep down into your long pockets
              He's no stranger to perpetrating unspeakable things
                  The tales he's told me practically
                  Popped my eyes from their sockets

                        So, without further ado
                        Let me introduce to you
                        Desmond the Decapitator
                        Who's going to bring us
                        The head of Albert Draper.'

Big Orange Quiet Sky

Can you hear the silence?
A thick blanket of hush
Mutes the crystal January fields
And a single twig snap
Turns the treble ironically up
Making a brittle drama of
A broken branch.

Can you smell burning?
The sunset ablaze from end to end
The blinding horizon slowly reduces
To a cinder
Leaving so many hot colours behind
Until blackness falls
Without a sound
Adding weight to the silence.

For Bill

It's Not Like Withering-by-the-Sea

I don't often complain
Complaining's just not me
But this holiday's been almost pleasant
It's not like Withering-by-the-Sea

For a start, the room is disturbingly clean
And all the appliances work
And you can't smoke anywhere on the premises
It's not like Withering-by-the-Sea
You could set fire to your bed for all they cared
They'd just claim on their dodgy insurance policy
And have a fire damage sale in the car park
In the Sunday morning boot fair

And the sun's been shining every bloody day
And the sea here's for swimming, not dumping
I'm not being funny, but I have to say
That's nothing like Withering-by-the-Sea

And the staff are all friendly
Not surly and uncommunicative
And they're always there
They don't disappear like Granddad's whisky
(It was the babysitter, I swear
I never trusted that fella)
And all the food's cooked properly
And the eggs don't give you salmonella
It's definitely not like Withering-by-the-Sea

We'll not be coming back
Holidays are for enduring, not enjoying.

Silent Reflection

This is
A moment of silent reflection
When insomniac fish hold their breath
For fear of rippling
Not a fin twitches
No bubbles escape
Pond skaters unboot and
No longer bound by surface tension
Slide like string to the river bottom
Water boatmen hold their oars aloft
All motionless beneath the silvered surface
Just an instant of silent reflection
The apogee of a breath's orbit
The furthest point between
Out and in
A frozen trice, just there.

The Difficult Patient, Sidebar:

Desmond Appleby was a middle child
Blamed for every fight, every broken cup
Yet his smile and his manner were always so mild
Like Larkin's piece about those who fuck you up
It could be that Desmond's parents were a contributory factor

From an early age, he was a convincing actor
Unnervingly pleasant and terrifyingly nice
He progressed through each chapter of the serial killer fable
As he pulled the wings from moths and the legs off mice
Beat his little brother's hamster to jam
With a cane as soon as he was able
Then turned an eager eye to the former hamster's owner

And after a freak mishap involving a loose trainer wheel
In the relentless path of a runaway steamroller
His grieving parents were grateful that Desmond kept it real
His elder brother crying on his shoulder
But really, his feelings couldn't have been colder
His friends and peers thought him quite manly
Though in his head he was stifling a smile
At the ironic destruction of his little sibling, Stanley.

About Desmond

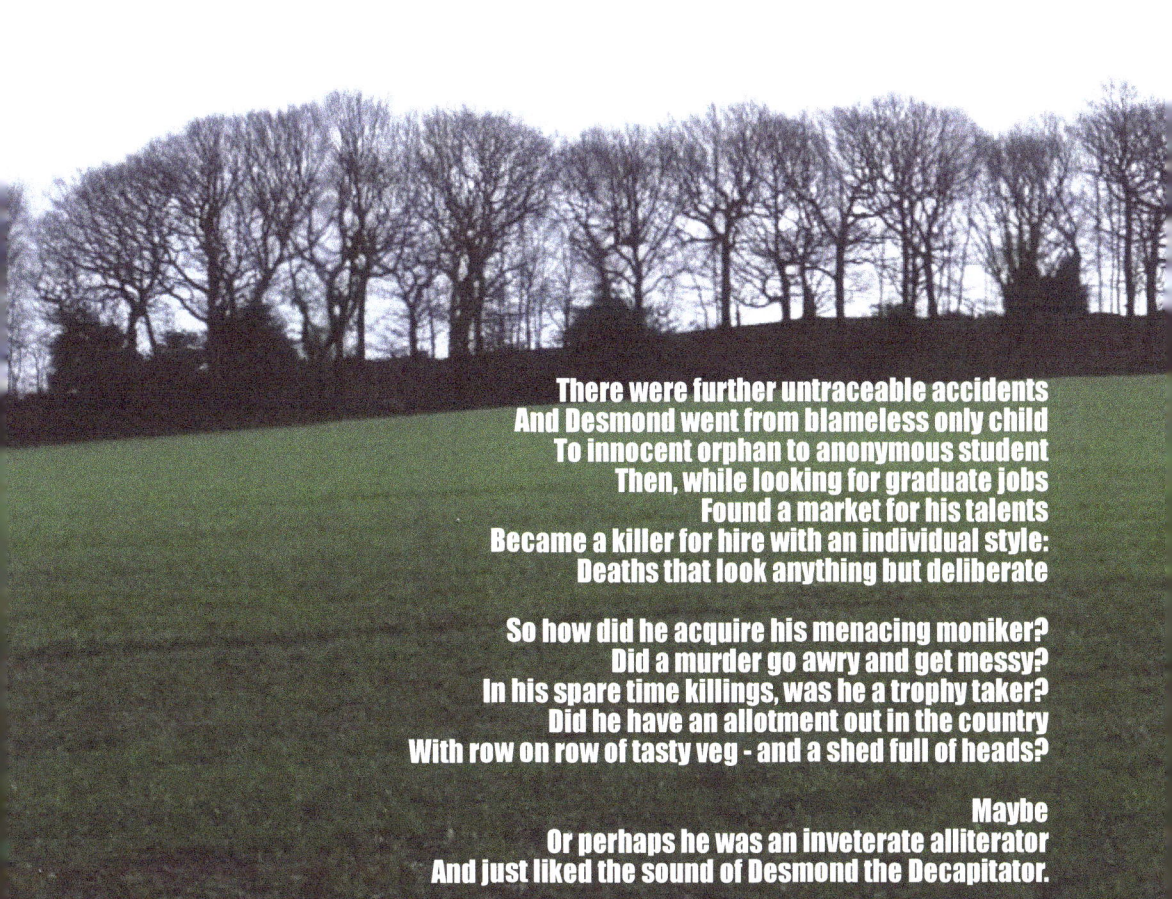

There were further untraceable accidents
And Desmond went from blameless only child
To innocent orphan to anonymous student
Then, while looking for graduate jobs
Found a market for his talents
Became a killer for hire with an individual style:
Deaths that look anything but deliberate

So how did he acquire his menacing moniker?
Did a murder go awry and get messy?
In his spare time killings, was he a trophy taker?
Did he have an allotment out in the country
With row on row of tasty veg - and a shed full of heads?

Maybe
Or perhaps he was an inveterate alliterator
And just liked the sound of Desmond the Decapitator.

Dark Presses Down

Some days you can't shake
Whelming existential dread
As dark presses down
Wait a while and it will pass
All troughs become peaks in time

Unfamiliar

I don't remember
Walking this vein-shadowed path
It's not the way home
I wonder where it will lead
Far too late to turn back now

Appointment With

Some weekends when I was a kid
I used to stay with my Grandma
And she used to let me stay up
Curled up snug on the settee to
Watch horror films in black and white:
Zombies, vampires, werewolves and witches
Grandma snoring in her armchair.

Lock all your doors and windows
The announcer would always say
It's Friday
It's time for
Appointment With Fear

Meanwhile, back on the settee
I simply could not fall asleep
The excitement of a ten year-old
The dry-mouthed anticipation
The waiting weightlessness, floating
Over the fathomless feather-lined pit of my stomach
Poised at the brow, and just before the vertiginous drop
Into a rollercoaster ride through the lands of
Universal, Hammer, Amicus and Trigon and such
With the witty and urbane double act Cushing and Lee,
Lon Chaney Jr, the son of the original Phantom of the Opera
And the Curse of the Werewolf with a cherubic Oliver Reed...

Fear

and my Grandma was nearly always asleep twenty minutes in
But even if she didn't nod off, nothing ever scared her
Films were just pictures, books were just words
Neither of them could hurt her
Or me
Or so she said
With laconic but firm reassurance
When I woke, wailing, at a vision of the wide-eyed woman from Witchcraft
'She'll not hurt you.'
Unmoved she was by reading the books I got from the adult library
(The children's section could no longer contain me)
Unbothered by Elliot O'Donnell's Screaming Skulls
Unshaken by the true tales of supernatural retribution
In his Casebook of Ghosts
Despite my mother's misgivings
'Oooh it'll not hurt him.'

My Grandma was not scared by anything
Except, perhaps, James Herbert's The Rats
Which she read, cover-to-cover in a night
Then next morning, her face somewhere
Between a grin and a grimace
She said:
'Every time I was dropping off
I could see their little red eyes
Staring back at me
From the bottom of the bed.'

The Difficult Patient, part eight

Albert Draper spent a long time in his long life
Loving nobody, not even himself
Couldn't see the profit in either a husband or a wife
So rather than being left there
He actively sought out and built a mansion on the shelf
Found a kind of angrily resigned solace in solitude
Until Imogen Smart knocked on his door.

Imogen Smart never really had time for love
Her heart's diary was always full of blank paper
For so many years, being paid to care seemed enough
But there was something about Mr Draper
Something about his wily, wise, wizened face
And the simple fun they enjoyed every day
That made her eyes shine and her heart sing.

So while it was true
That individually
They were relentless
One thing they'd both given up
Was a life of loneliness

Vixen, Captured

Coat puffed out
Against the bite
Of the midwinter air
Her eyes blaze
Captured by a flash
Of light no human sees
She stares, enraptured
Into that non-light
For a second or two
Before returning to
Her night duties

Summat in Miss Dale's

This really happened
On a bitter, starless February night
Making stuff for bright, bold patches
To go on my crisp green Woodcraft shirt
And singing Green Grow the Rushes-o
(I'll give you one-O!)
On account of our usual venue
Being used for something grown-up
And boring

In my junior school hall
Bigger in the dark
The stage in shadow
Billowing curtains
Where last autumn I had been 'Potiphar -
Yeoman of the Guard
To the great King Joseph!'
And Mrs S Jones
Despaired of my flattened vowels.

(Years later, I returned to that stage
As a full-grown actor in my first job
And tears fell as a beaming Mrs S Jones
Said 'Well done! Oh, well done!')

Classroom

Anyway, me and my mate Neville Stokes
Were busting for a pee
And busting to see
Our school from the inside
In the dark
What an adventure!

    So we asked the leader
    (Our next door neighbour, by the way)
    Who rejoiced in the name Beat Keyworth
    And her lanky son John, also a leader,
    With equine features
    And a dome like Bobby Charlton
    Put the corridor lights on
    So we could see our way to the toilets
    And told us not to be too long
    No messing about! And don't forget
    To wash your hands!
    Oh never mind

        Nodding, not listening, we were off!
        Try to stop us!
        Scuttling down the corridor
        All knees and elbows
        Practically running up the walls
        Like motorbikers on the Wall of
        Death
        From under the clock
        Where you had to stand
        If you'd got done
        Down past the girls' cloakroom
        To the boys' bogs
        For a quick wee and then back
        To making stuff for patches

Summat in Miss Dale's

But no
Cos Neville was standing stock still
Staring
At the part of the corridor
That remained stubbornly unlit
And at the end
Miss Dale's classroom
Right at the end

And Neville said:

'I dare you! I dare you to go down
To the bottom
To Miss Dale's
And try the door.
I dare you. Or are you yitten?'

Well, I had to do it, didn't I?
I started off walking
But as it got darker
My feet got faster
And then

AND THEN

Miss Dale's classroom door
Opened and slammed shut
Like a gunshot
Like a glass and metal drum
Booming in the bitter night
I yelped and fled back to the light
To Neville's face - a pale O of shock

Classroom

And we were shouting as we
Burst back in the hall
Everyone looking up from their crafts
'There's summat in Miss Dale's classroom!
Summat slammed the door!'
'Probably the wind.' was Beat's
Sage proclamation
As she escorted us down the now
Fully-lit corridor and tried
Miss Dale's door - and of course
Of course
It was locked
'But, but...'
And then it was John with:
'That's enough of your nonsense.
Scaring the Elfins!'
Who were, of course, crying by this time.
'But honest, John!
Honest!
There were summat there!'

And I recounted this tale
Recently to my mother
Who had no recollection of this event
But she revealed a little nugget of
Background information about
My old junior school
Cos back in the day
One of the workmen
When it was being built
There was an incident
A terrible accident
And one of the workmen
Was killed.
So maybe
Just maybe.
But really, it was probably just the wind.
Probably.

Burnt-Out Life

I'm a drive-by drama on a cold starless night
I'm crying on the pavement in my curlers and slippers
I'm spitty screaming drunks in a countryside campsite
I'm the guy upstairs who cremated his kippers
I'm the blazing row that ends in an arrest
I lost my wallet and look, I'm no nutcase
I'm beyond suspicion - I just need twenty quid

I'm the bastard who nicked his suitcase
Found laptopless and conked in a skip
I'm the smouldering ciggie on a sleeping chest
I'm the forensics team sifting through the ashes
For evidence of foul play

But kids did it, kids with accelerant and matches
No-one would have insurance for somewhere like this
I'm the burnt-out life
The remains of nothing in particular
That nobody will miss

The Difficult Patient, part nine

Neither bride nor groom
Had any family to speak of
At least, none still here
And the witness was some random chap
The registrar had collared en route
All things considered
It wasn't exactly the wedding of the year

The ceremony took place in Mr Draper's bedroom
It had been the extent of his world for many a year
He wore his very best false teeth
And was seated in a shiny new wheelchair
Specially delivered for the occasion
She was resplendent in medical green
Her dear departed mother would have shed a tear

The ceremony was brief to the point of rudeness
'Do you?' 'Yes!' 'What about you?' 'What do you think?'
She bent to kiss him and after, he said, mildly vexed:
'I love you, Imogen, but get the telly on
Otherwise we'll miss the 2:30 from Catterick
And the winner you picked will come in unwatched.'

But before they went on to enjoy
Their virtual honeymoon at the races
They had a legal obligation
To sign the register, to prove they were spouses
And the witness
His smile and his manner so mild
Was none other than the bookies' assassin
Who had just realised, his heart beating wild
That he may have been aimed at the wrong target.

Dizzy Heights

The dream I sometimes had as a child
Standing at the top of the stairs
In the flat-roofed cube of my first childhood home
Standing, ready in soft pyjamas
My pudgy little toes
Overhanging the top step
Wriggling and wiggling and ready
And then
Oh, and then
Then I jump without hesitation
From the top of the stairs
And hanging on to the bannister
My feet swing up behind me
Like the blank white cottage cheese
Polystyrene bricks
In Chapeltown baths
Buoyant, bobbing, unstoppable
And I pull myself down
Hand over hand
Feet still floating, trailing like streamers
Like banners, rippling, flapping
Ages pass
The light changes
Becomes thicker, darker
And I am float/fly/drifting in the hall
And I see me
In my soft pyjamas
In the ornate hall mirror
Waving back at me
As I pass
And I never, ever land
Never.

inbetween

this is a place for
shifty lookers to lurk
in clandestine conclaves
where the reverberation of
rumbly, fumbly jangly guitaring
& sandpapery-voiced singing rings
for tear-smeared shouters after the
pubs are long-closed & the niteclubs are
kicking out the sad stragglers & the lost souls
this is a place where we're neither here nor there

this is inbetween

Moita Negra Midwinter Night

Sharp night air cuts with a frosted scythe;
A loose necklace of lonely streetlamps
Burns orange bright, makes blacks blacker, dark starker;
Eager howls, full of the unfulfilled promise of the hunt
Echo in the lightless valley,
Barking and whining as the boar tease past their kennels;
Owls agree to disagree, they pause, then agree to disagree again;
A nightjar gurgles and gargles, a slow, strangled siren.
No human walks out this night -
This Moita Negra midwinter night.

She guided his suddenly shaky hand
And they smiled as he scrawled under her scrawl
Then it was all over bar the witnessing
After which the witness smiled too
And said to everyone present:
'This has all been a terrible mistake,
And now I can't let anyone leave here
Not alive.'

As slick and quick as the click of a ballpoint
Desmond withdrew his katana
At the sight of the blade
Mr Draper did something he'd never done before:
He gave up.
Or at least his heart did.

Leaving Imogen hunched over his still form, inconsolate
Holding his sparsely-haired head in an awkward pietá

'Well this whole episode has been
Somewhat precipitous and unexpected.'
And with a swish of steel
Left the registrar clutching her throat
As life left in a rush.
Desmond could plainly see Imogen's hurt

He spoke softly, with regret
While cleaning his blade in the crook of his elbow
'At untraceable murder I'm usually expert
I was waiting to poison the catering, you see
But this nice lady asked me to be your witness
And I'm too nice for my own good.
Ah well
I suppose this has saved me the trouble.

'I can't shake the feeling that
You should be the one I'm after
But clients are daft, generally
And this lot are dafter
Anyway, I hate to be heartless
But now that he's dead
I don't suppose you'll be needing his head?'

Shot

Many times
Nothing walks past the forest camera
And it captures the moment
Perfectly.

The Optimist

I'll wait, just in case
The chef sees my hungry face
There's always the chance
The faint possibility
The guests won't need all the fish.

A Gentle Legacy

To be the laughter dancing in the eyes
The affable promise of mischief
The fun just round the corner
To be the bringer of sunshine
The trusted pair of hands
The warmth in the room
To be held kindly in everyone's hearts
The last good word on the lips
The hug on the steps
At the end of the night
Leaving behind
A gentle legacy.

The Difficult Patient, part eleven

Desmond Appleby awoke kneeling
With a crashing headache
And his hands zip-tied behind his back
He was careful to keep his muscles slack
As he formulated a plan of escape

Behind him, beyond his peripheral vision
Imogen spoke:
'It's not fair, what you've done here
He was an absolute pain,
But he was my absolute pain
I wasn't in it for the money, I'd made it my mission
To demonstrate to him what it was like to care
And it took a while - nearly drove me insane

'But I never gave up. It's how I got this job
I was persistently kind, and slowly, so slowly
Mr Draper learned how to love.

'Oh, nothing physical! Don't start me laughing!
At his age, he could barely raise a smile
And me, I've never been bothered
Not really my thing.

Neither am I one for scintillating jewels
Or any sort of designer schmutter
Anyway, I bet you're wondering
What set us down the path of true love?
It was when
We discovered we both liked a flutter.'

'Mmmf' said Desmond around the hankie
Imogen had used as a makeshift gag
She continued:
'I've had this talent all my life
Picking out the horses is child's play for me.

So I'm keeping some of the winnings
After all, however briefly, I was his wife
But I'll give 'em some back, 'cos frankly
Hoarding a fortune's not really my bag
So the bookies will be happy, unlike me.

'And as for you, my would-be assassin
You've ruined my life
You took away the only human
That I didn't hate
And there's no point in struggling
Not now, it's too late.'

'Mmmf' said Desmond again
As he heard the swish of the katana
Then the ground rushed up to meet him
But by the time he kissed it
He was a goner.

She Flies Alone

She takes her own sweet time
She will not be pushed
She starts when she is ready
She might listen attentively
But she will not be rushed
Last on the bus and first in the bar
Loves the train and hates the car
She likes her life the way it is
She soars above the rest of us
Effortless
She flies alone
And that's just the way she wants it.

For Clare

Always good to know
Even when you're not around
Still you're somewhere inside
Singing sweet in their heart's space
A tune they cannot forget.

Still There

Quinta da Silva

'Who'd want to farm brambles?'
Lucy laughed as she dragged
A flaccid pink velour airbed
From the womb of their powder blue Dormobile
Onto the dusty floor
Of their newly-adopted home
Kilometres from anywhere
But pretty close to the middle of
Portuguese nowhere.

'Maybe they used to make blackberry wine.'
Dominic shrugged as he stomped the pump
Into humming life
And they spent a first fitful night by camping nightlight
Watching agog as a Moorish gecko
Licking a dusty eye
Zigzagged up a rustic bedroom wall
Shrieking hilariously at house centipedes
With far too many legs
Bombing and skittering across the russet tiles

And eventually
Dreaming of thorns
Pulling and tearing
Hooking and digging in
And blood
So. Much. Blood.

One bad dream doesn't spoil
A whole summer
Even if Lu and Dom
Had exactly the same one
They never even discussed it
(Neither Dom nor Lu
Were the dream sharing type)

But they were busy
Living their best life
Under a beautiful blazing sun
In a kitten-eye blue sky
Peachy pink sunsets
And a moon so bright
You could read a book by its light

Dominic spent his days
Swinging his braying petrol strimmer
Through tight spirals of thick bramble
Or silva, as he Google Translated
(Too shy to ask the sparse neighbours)

Quinta da Silva

Lucy tried her hand at cutting new paths
Through the eye-high, weed-suffocated valley
Up to the forest beyond
But retreated, weeping and bleeding
Ripping herself from the silva's
Thorny embrace.

After that
She left Dominic to it.

Long day followed brief night followed long day
And no matter how much time Dominic spent
Cutting through swathes of silva-swamped land
Next morning bright and early
The brambles were back
Taller and thicker and lusher and pricklier than ever
And closer, ever closer
To their neat little farmhouse
With the central door
And the windows one, two, three, four
Just like the Play School drawing of a house
From their BBC television childhood

And one arid afternoon
Lucy swore she saw
A distant neighbour's stray goat
Nonchalantly munching
On some plump, purple blooded, bulbous blackberries
Only to be silently hooked by stealthy, snaky tendrils
Bound by a muzzle of thorns
And dragged inexorably into the silva's spiny maw
Which snapped shut, toxic and tight
As if nothing untoward had happened

Quinta da Silva

Nobody believed her

They didn't believe her
When she called the police
In badly broken Portuguese
Because a few days previous,
Dom had gone out
To find the goat
That she had told him about
And he was still out there.

They didn't believe her
When she told them their
Powder-blue Dormobile
Somehow had four flat tyres
And that she'd watched aghast
As the silva slithered into the gas tank
Strangling the engine
And still no sign of Dominic

But her mother believed her
When she used her mobile's last gasp
When she wept down the airwaves
That she was trapped in the
Neat little farmhouse
Because the brambles had grown over every exit
Every cute little square window
Had pinned the Moorish gecko to the wall
Like a museum exhibit
Pierced its dusty eye

And she was entombed in a greenlit, rustling cave
'I can feel it, Mum, strangling my home
Squeezing through the brickwork

Displacing the foundations
Pushing through the grey grout
Between the russet floor tiles
And I want my Dom back!'

And one morning
When Lucy's mother
And the local cops
Turned up at Quinta da Silva
They found the overgrown wreck of a camper van

And where once there was
A neat little farmhouse
With a central door
And windows one, two, three, four
Now all there was
Was silva.

Quinta da Silva

Luv Vincent Parrot, Season Finale

Dry-eyed and purposeful
Imogen made a call late that drizzly night
On a disposable, untraceable mobile
She bought from a stall in the covered market.

'You don't know me, Bettie Spender
But I know you
Now I'm not the sort to repeat herself
So you'd best take notice.

I've got bad news and worse news
The bad news is your attempt at assassination
Was anything but a success
The worse news is your hitman
Killed the wrong people
Made a terrible mess
Pretty poor for a perfect murderer
Wouldn't you say? I guess
There's no other way of putting this
He kind of lost his head.

'But don't worry
I took it with me.

'I'm going to leave it in the doorway
Of your son's money-laundering café
Safely wrapped up in a bright green bin bag
With a fat roll of notes in his gob
For an apple like the pig he was.

'Don't come after me, Bettie
I can guarantee that if you do
You'll always be looking over your shoulder
Cos I'll be coming after you
I've got your killer's Samurai sword
And you can take me at my word
I never give up.'

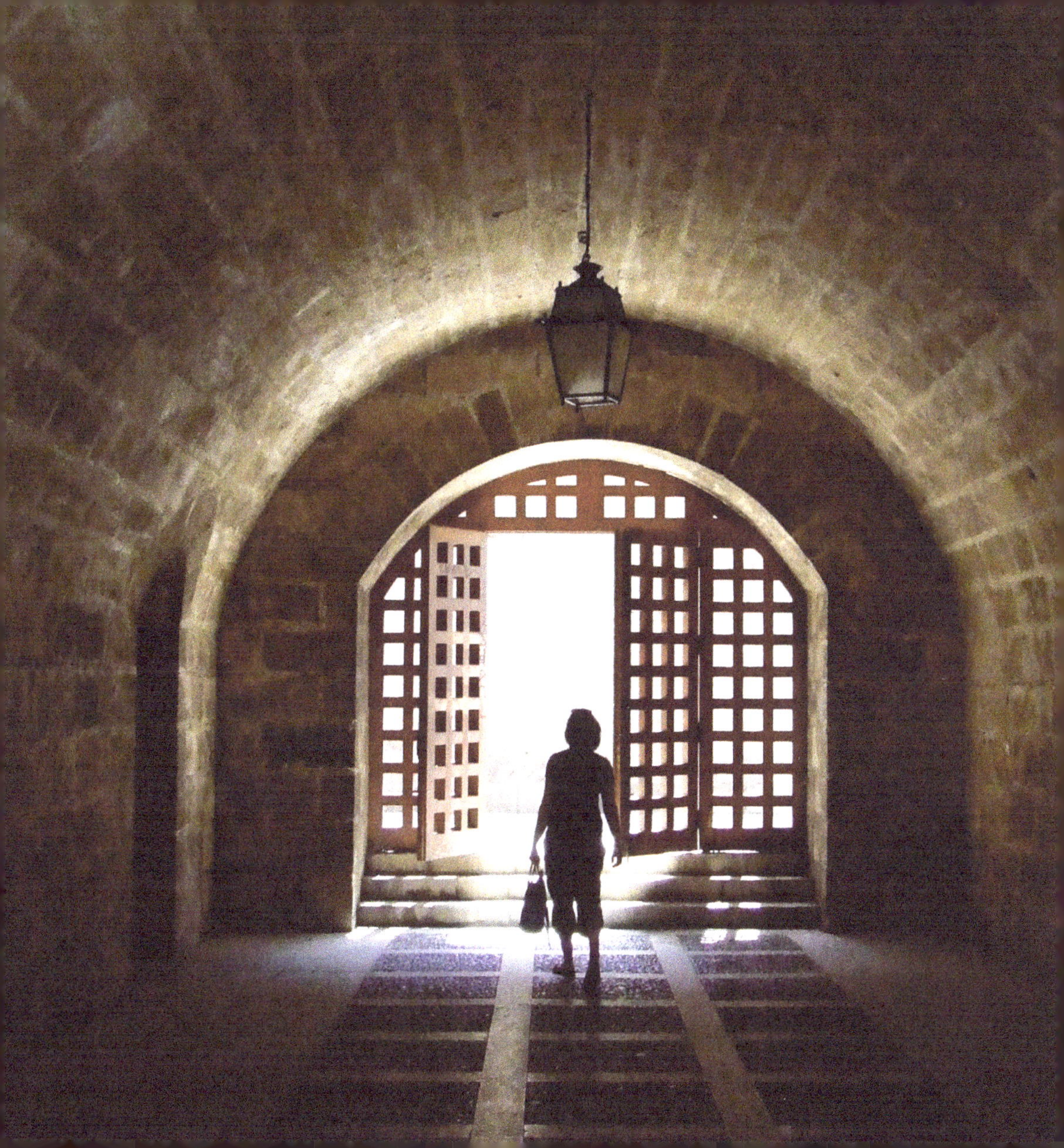

The Party's Over

The air has been kissed to unfulfillment
The balloons are all wrinkly and deflated
The promise of a great time has all been spent
Sparklers extinguished, confetti unfettered,
Poppers popped, streamers soggy and bleeding
Multicolours on blank tablecloths
Bottles emptied, champers flat,
The barstaff pale and hungover
One last guest appeared
From under a table
Stretched, yawned and blinkingly asked
'Is the party over?'

What Do We Leave Behind?

What do we leave behind?
Photo albums crammed with family snaps, some bad
Here with Gran on the beach in black and white
There at a party in the youth club one night
Christmases and christenings and weddings
Rows and rows and piles of books, most read
The one lent out to someone who lost touch
The last part of a series left on the bus
Diaries, notebooks full of appointments and musings
And the trophies and the baby clothes
And the ornaments and endless paperwork
And the shells from that beach, still in Gran's hanky
And the first kiss outside, after the party
And the loved ones, the family and friends
And the memories, sweet and not so
And the bad and the fun times
And the tears
And the love
All left behind.

I've Been Out

Where have I been?
I have been on a venture
I was chasing after chasers
Or being chased around
The details become sketchier
The more I try to pin them down

Where have I been?
I'm sad it's over
But the things I've seen
There's no point
In trying to explain
You wouldn't understand
And none of it was planned

Where have I been?
You keep asking me that
I don't have an answer
All you need to know
Is that I've been out
And now I'm back
Did you miss me?

Millhouse Davis-Kurley
2002-2021

Without Words

Without the words
a novel is just a notebook
blank pages
full of potential
countries unexplored
dramas unplayed
loves undiscovered
worlds undreamt
conflicts unfought
endings yet to be met.

Acknowledgements

Thank you to:
My friend and mentor, Kate Hull Rodgers; Bill Rodgers for years of encouragement; Tony Gardner, for unflinching editorial assistance (he's gonna hate all these semi-colons); and of course, The Lovely Ali, for putting up with me.

'What Do We Leave Behind?' is also published in The Lock Down Legacy, booklet three.

'I Told You There Was a Wolf' came third in the Slipstream Poets Open Poetry Competition 2021.

The Difficult Patient, Post-Credits Scene: Some Party

Her trainer-socked foot in a puddle
Jump-started her early morning, alone and cold
In the pissy doorway of some insolvent café
Last night was a jumbled jigsaw
Corners and edges and
The odd bit in the middle were missing
As was her handbag
With her life, her identity
Her everything
In it
She was wearing a mystery trenchcoat
And at least her other shoe
Was in the next doorway
So not all bad
So far
Perhaps the contents
Of the bright green bin bag
That had served as a pillow
Could furnish her with some missing pieces
However
A fat roll of bloodstained banknotes
And a stranger's severed head
Provided more questions than answers
Or he would
Were he still attached
To the rest of him.

Lightning Source UK Ltd.
Milton Keynes UK
UKHW050728220922
409254UK00003B/23

9 781803 694276